Everybody's Favorite Series No. 1

Everybody's Favorite Songs

FOREWORD This book is respectfully dedicated to the music loving public of the world by the publishers who sincerely believe it represents a complete musical encyclopedia, and fills a long felt need. We trust it will bring many happy hours of musical entertainment.

THE EDITOR

Order No. AM 40007
US International Standard Book Number: 0.8256.2001.5
UK International Standard Book Number: 0.7119.0427.8

Exclusive Distributors:
Music Sales Corporation
257 Park Avenue South, New York, NY 10010 USA
Music Sales Limited
8/9 Frith Street, London W1V 5TZ England
Music Sales Pty. Limited
120 Rothschild Street, Rosebery, Sydney, NSW 2018, Australia

Printed in the United States of America by
Vicks Lithograph and Printing Corporation

CONTENTS

CLASSIFIED INDEX

Songs Arranged for the following instruments and voice:

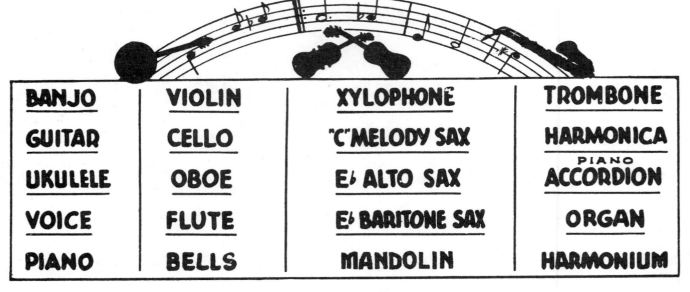

BANJO	VIOLIN	XYLOPHONE	TROMBONE
GUITAR	CELLO	"C" MELODY SAX	HARMONICA
UKULELE	OBOE	Eb ALTO SAX	PIANO ACCORDION
VOICE	FLUTE	Eb BARITONE SAX	ORGAN
PIANO	BELLS	MANDOLIN	HARMONIUM

ARRANGEMENT CHART

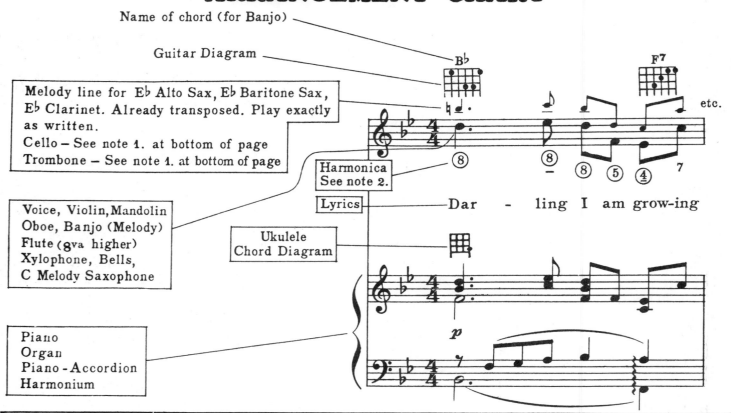

Name of chord (for Banjo)

Guitar Diagram

Melody line for Eb Alto Sax, Eb Baritone Sax, Eb Clarinet. Already transposed. Play exactly as written.
Cello – See note 1. at bottom of page
Trombone – See note 1. at bottom of page

Harmonica See note 2.

Lyrics

Voice, Violin, Mandolin Oboe, Banjo (Melody) Flute (8va higher) Xylophone, Bells, C Melody Saxophone

Ukulele Chord Diagram

Piano Organ Piano - Accordion Harmonium

Dar - ling I am grow-ing

NOTE 1. – For Cello or Trombone – Read upper (small) notes as if written in the Bass clef (𝄢). If both the upper and lower notes are preceded by accidentals (sharps or flats) use the accidental preceding the lower note. If only the upper note is preceded by an accidental, disregard the accidental.

NOTE 2. – In the Harmonica arrangement, the numbers represent the holes on the Hohner harmonica – The numbers without circles represent notes played by blowing the breath. The numbers with circles represent notes played by drawing the breath. A dash under a note means to play that note one-half tone higher.

Beautiful Blue Danube

Lyric by
KERMIT LYONS
Arrgt. by Paul Hill

Music by
JOHANN STRAUSS

Élégie

Lyric by
KERMIT LYONS

Music by
JULES M. MASSENET

(cont'd)

Till she re - turns ____ My heart yearns, ___ Oh, Blue Dan - ube, Bring her home. ____

Ev-'ry night finds me all a - lone love dreams have flown

Dark-ness drags my heart down low, No light shines to show the way where is the day

Sun would bring so - lace I know. Once my poor heart sang love's re-frain ____ Spring-time was

In Old Madrid

Words by
CLIFTON BINGHAM
Arr. by Paul Hill

Music by
H. TROTERE

Tune Uke

F Bb D G

I Love You Truly

To A. B. H.

Words and Music by
CARRIE JACOBS-BOND

Santa Lucia

Italian Folk Song

Gone is the sor-row, Gone doubt and fear, For you love me tru-ly, tru-ly, dear.

Tune Uke

G C E A

1. O'er sea the sil-ver star bright light is throw-ing, Hushed now the
2. See how the balm-y breeze our sails ex-pand-ing, Naught could our

bil-lows are gen-tle winds blow-ing; Come to my bark with me,
hearts more please on this winds deck stand-ing, Come, trav-'lers, one and all,

Come sail a-cross the sea, San-ta Lu-ci-a, San-ta Lu-ci-a.
Come quick-ly to my call, San-ta Lu-ci-a, San-ta Lu-ci-a.

Melody in F

Arrgt. by Paul Hill

A. RUBINSTEIN

Ben Bolt
(Sweet Alice)

Arr. by Paul Hill

J. KNEASS

Oh! don't you re-mem-ber sweet Al-ice Ben Bolt Sweet Al-ice with hair so
Oh! don't you re-mem-ber the wood Ben Bolt Near the green sun-ny slope of the

brown She wept with de-light when you gave her a smile And trem-bled with fear at your
hill When oft we have sung near it's wide spread ing shade And kept time to the click of the

frown. In the old church-yard in the val-ley Ben Bolt In a cor-ner ob-scure and a-
mill. The mill has gone to de-cay Ben Bolt And a qui-et now reigns all a-

lone ____ They have fit-ted a slab of gran-ite so gray And sweet Al-ice lies un-der the
round ____ See the old rus-tic porch with it's ro-ses so sweet Lies scat-terd and fall'n to the

stone They have fit-ted a slab of gran-ite so gray And sweet Al-ice lies un-der the stone.
ground See the old rus-tic porch with it's ro-ses so sweet Lies scat-terd and fall'n to the ground.

A Song Of India

Lyric by
KERMIT LYONS
Arrgt. by Paul Hill

N. RIMSKY-KORSAKOV

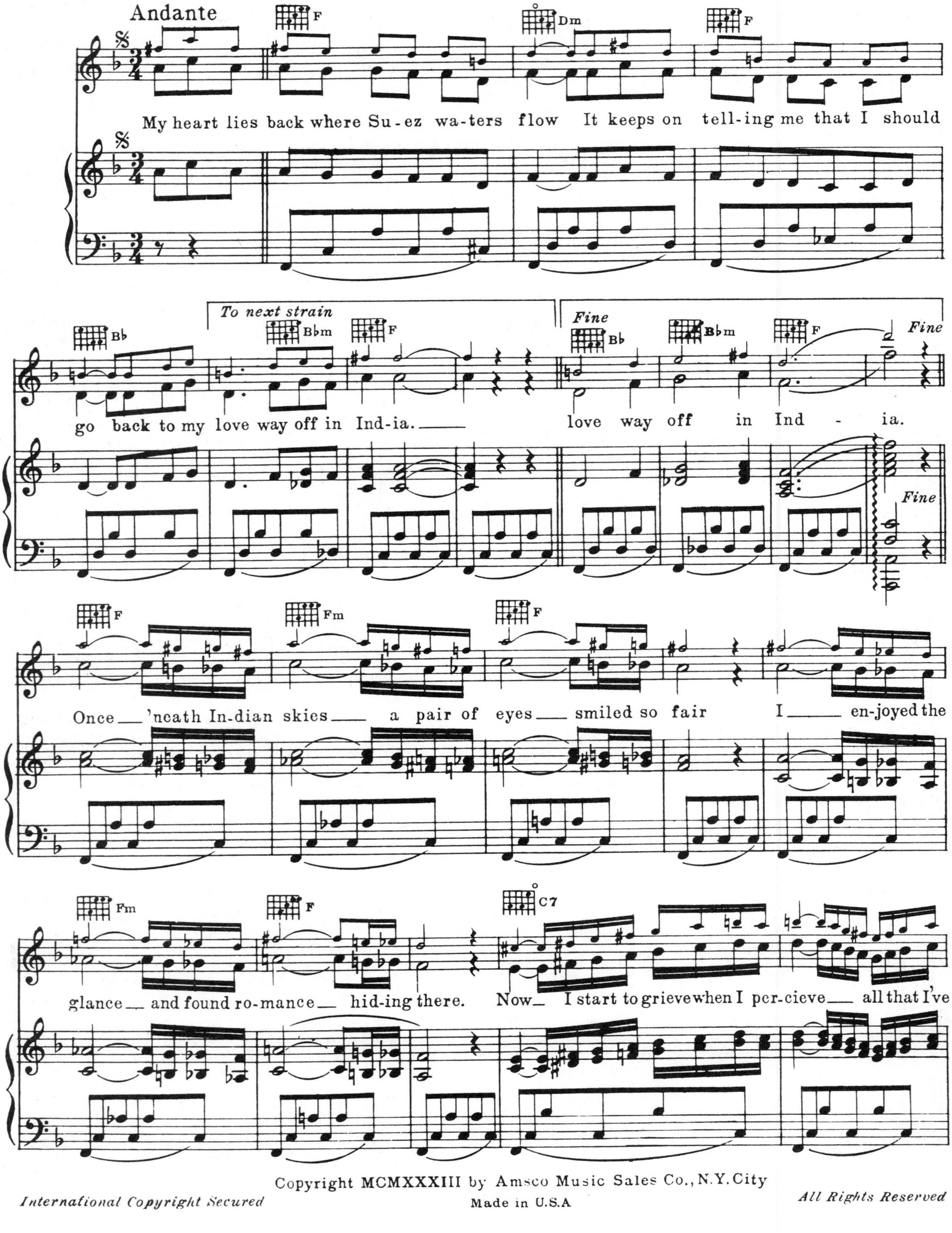

Andante
F
Dm
F
My heart lies back where Su-ez wa-ters flow It keeps on tell-ing me that I should
Bb
To next strain
Bbm
F
Fine
Bb
Bbm
F
Fine
go back to my love way off in Ind-ia.
love way off in Ind - ia.
Fine
F
Fm
F
Once 'neath In-dian skies a pair of eyes smiled so fair I en-joyed the
Fm
F
C7
glance and found ro-mance hid-ing there. Now I start to grieve when I per-cieve all that I've

15

A Song Of India-2

Serenade

Lyric by
KERMIT LYONS
Arrgt. by Paul Hill

FRANZ SCHUBERT

Wedding March
(Midsummer Night's Dream)

Words by
KERMIT LYONS
Arrgt. by Paul Hill

F. MENDELSSOHN

Moderato

Ding, Dong, the or-gan swells with tones so deep to-day
Ding, Dong, the chimes ring out and seem to the world to say

Ding, Dong, the or-gan tells of two hearts bright and gay
Ding, Dong, the chimes sing out that this is a wed-ding day

Fine

Two loves will soon be joined Two lives will soon have learned, That life is good and that On-ly true love makes the world worth while.

D.S. al Fine

Cradle Song
(Wiegenlied)

Arrgt. by Paul Hill

JOHANNES BRAHMS

Valse Andante

Lul-la-by and good-night, with ros-es be dight, with lil-ies be-decked is ba-by's wee bed; Lay thee

down now and rest, May thy slum-ber be blest, Lay thee down now and rest, May thy slum-ber be blest.

The Loreley

Arrgt. by Paul Hill

F. SILCHER

1. I know not what spell is en-chant-ing, That makes me sad-ly in-clined __ An
2. The fair - est maid is en-clin-ing, In daz-zling beau-ty there, __ Her

old strange leg-end is haunt-ing And will not leave my mind ____ The
gild-ed rai-ment is shin-ing She combs her gold-en hair, ____ With

day-light slow-ly is go-ing and calm-ly flows the Rhine ____ The
gold-en comb she's comb-ing and as she combs she sings ____ Her

moun-tain's peak is glow-ing In eve-ning's mel-low shine. ____
song a-midst the gloam-ing, A weird en-chant-ment brings. ____

Hark, Hark, The Lark

Arrgt. by Paul Hill

FRANZ SCHUBERT

On Wings Of Song

F. MENDELSSOHN

Andante tranquillo

1. I'll bear thee off, my dear - est, Up - on the wings of my
2. vio - lets whisper to - geth - er, And peek at the stars from their

song, Off to a spot that I know of, Where Gan - ges rolls a - long. For
dell, And there to each oth-er the ros - es Their sweet-scent-ed fairy tales tell. The

there in a beau-ti-ful gar - den, While Cyn - thia rides in state,____ The lo - tus-blos-soms for
dain-ty ga-zelles will lis - ten, And cau-tious-ly ex - plore,____ While aye is heard in the

thee, dear, Their dar - ling sis - ter, wait.____ The lo - tus-blos-soms for thee,____
dis - tance The sa - cred riv - er's roar,____ While aye is heard in the dis - - -

Humoresque

Lyric by
KERMIT LYONS
Arrgt. by Paul Hill

Music by
ANTON DVORAK

Hu-mo-resque, my heart's at rest for when I hear your tones so clear they sing of peace, all worries cease for me. Mel-o-dy you bring to me a mem-o-ry that seems to be so real it's all so plain to see.

Home and a moon-light, Love and a June night, that's the vi-sion oh, so plain And the breeze in the trees Sings the same mel-o-dies How I wish I could be there a-gain. *D.S. al Fine*

I'll Sing Thee Songs Of Araby

Arrgt. by Paul Hill

FREDERIC CLAY

Copyright MCMXXXIII by Amsco Music Sales Co., N.Y. City
Made in U.S.A.

Who Is Sylvia

By WILLIAM SHAKESPEARE
and FRANZ SCHUBERT

Arrgt. by Paul Hill

Drink To Me Only With Thine Eyes

Arrgt. by Paul Hill

BEN JONSON

Tune Uke

A D F♯ B

In The Evening By The Moonlight

By JAS. A. BLAND

I Cannot Sing The Old Songs

Arrgt. by Paul Hill

By CLARIBEL

Aloha Oe
Hawaiian Farewell Song

Arrgt. by Paul Hill

QUEEN LYDIA
KAMEKEHA LILIUOKALANI

Now has come the hour sad of part - ing, Our day dream of love, my own is o'er. On - ly
When you're far a - way, Ah, think of me, love, As I will be dreaming e'er of you. Let fond

mem - o - ries will soon be left us, Let our lives seem to glide on as be - fore, Fare-
re - col - lec - tions be your fan - cy, And to me may your heart be ev - er true.

well, dear love, I'll dream of you, No pass-ing grief is this my heart is feel - ing, I

love you so, be - fore you go, I'll say "Dear lov'd one fare - well."

Oh! Dem Golden Slippers

Tune Uke

A D F# B

Arrgt. by Paul Hill

CHORUS

Oh, dem gold-en slip-pers, Oh, dem gold-en slip-pers, gold-en slip-pers, I'se gwine to wear, Be-

kase dey look so neat Oh, dem gold-en slip-pers, Oh, dem gold-en slip-pers,

gold-en slip-pers I'se gwine to wear, To walk the gold-en street. street.

Oh! Dem Golden Slippers - 2

Silver Threads Among The Gold

Tune Uke
F Bb D G

Words by
E.E. REXFORD

Music by
H.P. DANKS
Arrgt. by Paul Hill

Silver Threads Among The Gold

D.S. al Fine

Old Folks At Home

Arrgt. by Paul Hill

By STEPHEN FOSTER

Sweet And Low

Arrgt. by Paul Hill

By J. BARNBY

Tune Uke
G C E A

Sweet and low, Sweet and low, Wind of the west - ern sea. _____
Sleep and rest, Sleep and rest, Fa - ther will come to thee soon. _____

Low, low_ breathe and blow Wind of the west - ern sea _____ O - ver the roll - ing
Rest, rest on moth - er's breast Fa - ther will come to thee soon _____ Fa - ther will come to his

wa - ters go, Come from the dy - ing moon_ and blow Blow him a - gain to
babe in the nest Sil - ver sails_ all out of the west Un - der the sil - ver

me _____ While my lit - tle one, While my pret - ty one sleeps. _____
moon Sleep my lit - tle one, Sleep my pret - ty one sleep. _____

Made in U.S.A.

Sally In Our Alley

Arrgt. by Paul Hill

HENRY CAREY

Sailing, Sailing

Arrgt. by Paul Hill

GODFREY MARKS

Old Oaken Bucket

SAMUEL WOODWORTH

Arrgt. by Paul Hill

When You And I Were Young, Maggie

Arrgt. by Paul Hill

By V. A. BUTTERFIELD

Tune Uke

G C E A

I wan-dered to-day to the hill, Mag-gie, To watch the scene be-low; The
They say I am fee-ble with age, Mag-gie, My steps less spright-ly than then; My

creek and the creak-ing old mill, Mag-gie, As we used to 'long long a go. The
face is a well writ-ten page, Mag-gie, But time a - lone was the pen. They

greengrove is gone from the hill, Mag-gie, Where first the dai - sies sprung, The
say we are a - ged and gray, Mag-gie, Spray by the white break-ers flung, But to

creak-ing old mill is still, Mag-gie, Since you and I were young.
me you're as fair as you were, Mag-gie, When you and I were young.

Made in U.S.A

Grandfather's Clock

Arrgt. by Paul Hill

By HENRY C. WORK

Oh! Susanna

Arrgt. by Paul Hill

By STEPHEN FOSTER

⁴²Believe Me If All Those Endearing Young Charms

THOMAS MOORE

Arrgt. by Paul Hill

Tune Uke
A D F♯ B

Be-lieve me if all those en-dear-ing young charms, Which I gaze on so fond-ly to-day.__ Were to

change by to-mor-row and flee from my arms; Like fair-y gifts fad-ing a-way__ Thou wouldst

still be a-dored, as this mo-ment thou art Let thy lov-li-ness fade as it will.__ And a-

round the dear ru-in, each wish of my heart, Would en-twine it-self ver-dant-ly still.__

Love's Old Sweet Song

Arrgt. by PAUL HILL

J. L. MOLLOY

Copyright MCMXXXII by Amsco Music Sales Co. N.Y. City
Made in U.S.A.

Emmett's Lullaby

Arrgt. by Paul Hill

J.K. EMMETT

Close your eyes Le - na my dar-ling while I sing your lu-la-by. Fear thou no dan-ger Le-na

Move not dear Le - na my dar-ling for your broth-er watch-es nigh you Le-na dear An-gels guide thee

Le-na dear my dar-ling noth-ing e - vil can come near. Bright-est flow-ers bloom for thee

dar - ling sis - ter, dear to me. Go to sleep, go to sleep, my ba - by, my ba - by, my ba - by

Go to sleep my ba - by; ba - by, oh, bye. Go to sleep Le - na sleep.

Roll On, Silver Moon

Arrgt. by Paul Hill

By J. W. TURNER

As I stray'd from my cot at the close of the day 'Mid the rav-ish-ing beau-ties of
As the hart on the moun-tain my lov-er was brave, So no-ble and man-ly and

June _ 'Neath a jess-a-mine shade I es-pied a fair maid and she plain-tive-ly sighed to the moon.
clev-er So kind and sin-cere, And he loved me full dear oh my Ed-win, his e-qual was nev-er.

Refrain

Roll on sil-ver moon guide the trav-'ler his way, While the night-in-gale's song is in tune; _ I

nev-er nev-er more with my true love will stray By the soft sil-ver beams, gen-tle moon.

Tune Uke
G C E A

Beautiful Dreamer

Arrgt. by Paul Hill

By STEPHEN FOSTER

Tune Uke
F Bb D G

Beau-ti-ful dream-er, wake un-to me,
Star-light and dew drops are wait-ing for thee,
Beau-ti-ful dream-er, out on the sea,
Mer-maids are chant-ing the wild lore - lei,

Sounds of the rude world heard in the day,
Lull'd by the moonlight have all passed a-way! Beau-ti-ful dream-er,
O - ver the stream-let, va-pors are born.
Wait-ing to fade at the bright coming morn. Beau-ti-ful dream-er,

Queen of my song,
List while I woo thee with soft mel-o-dy
Gone are the cares of
Beam of my heart,
E'en as the morn on the stream-let and sea.
Then will all clouds of

life's bus-y throng,
Beau-ti-ful dream-er a-wake un-to me.
sor-row de-part,
Beau-ti-ful dreamer a-wake un-to me.

Long, Long Ago

Arrgt. by Paul Hill

By THOMAS HAYNES BAYLY

Just Before The Battle, Mother

By GEO F. ROOT

Arrgt. by Paul Hill

Oh, you'll not for-get me, moth-er, If I'm num-bered with the slain.

Seeing Nellie Home
The Quilting Party

Arrgt. by Paul Hill

Moderato

Tune Uke

G C E A

In the sky the bright stars glit-tered ___ On the bank the pale moon shone And from Aunt Din-ah's

quilt-ing par-ty I was see - ing Nel-lie home, I was see-ing Nel-lie home.___ I was

see-ing Nel-lie home; And 'twas from Aunt Din-ah's quilt-ing par-ty I was see-ing Nel-lie home.

Songs My Mother Taught Me

51

In The Gloaming

Arrgt. by Paul Hill

By ANNIE F. HARRISON

When Johnny Comes Marching Home

Arrgt. by Paul Hill

L. LAMBERT

Tune Uke
G C E A

When John-ny comes marching home a - gain, Hur - rah! hur - rah! We'll give him a heart-y
The old church bell will peal with joy Hur - rah! hur - rah! To wel-come home our

wel - come then Hur - rah! — Hur - rah! — The men will cheer the boys will shout, The
dar - ling boy, Hur - rah! — Hur - rah! — The vil - lage lads and ass - ies say, With

lad - ies they will all turn out And we'll all feel gay When John-ny comes march-ing home. —
ros - es they will strew the way And we'll all feel gay When John-ny comes march-ing home. —

Sweet Genevieve

Arrgt. by Paul Hill

HENRY TUCKER

For He's A Jolly Good Fellow!

Arrgt. by Paul Hill

Listen To The Mocking Bird

Arrgt. by Paul Hill

ALICE HAWTHORNE

Made in U. S. A.

Chorus

Lis-ten to the mock-ing bird, Lis-ten to the mock-ing bird, The mock-ing bird, still sing-ing o'er her grave;

Lis-ten to the mock-ing bird, Lis-ten to the mock-ing bird, Still sing-ing where the weep-ing wil-lows wave.

Good Night Ladies

Arrgt. by Paul Hill

Tune Uke

F Bb D G

Good-night, lad-ies_ Good-night, lad-ies! Good-night, lad-ies We're going to leave you now.
Fare well, lad-ies_ Fare well, lad-ies! Fare well, lad-ies We're going to leave you now.
Sweet dreams, lad-ies_ Sweet dreams, lad-ies! Sweet dreams, lad-ies We're going to leave you now.

Allegro

Mer-ri-ly we roll a-long, Roll a-long, roll a-long, Mer-ri-ly we roll a-long, O'er the deep blue sea.

Darling Nelly Gray

Arrgt. by Paul Hill

B. R. HANDY

Made in U.S.A.

Home Sweet Home

Arrgt. by Paul Hill

By JOHN HOWARD PAYNE
and SIR HENRY BISHOP

sit-ting by the riv-er And I'm weep-ing all the day, For you've gone from the old Ken-tuck-y shore.

Tune Uke

F Bb D G

'Mid pleas-ures and pal-a-ces, tho' we may roam, Be it
ev-er so hum-ble, there's no place like home, A

charm from the skies seems to hal-low us there, Which,
seek thru the world is ne'er met with else where.

Home sweet home, Sweet home! There's no place like Home! Oh There is no place like home.

Whispering Hope

VOCAL DUET

ALICE HAWTHORNE

1. Soft as the voice of an an - gel, Breath-ing a les-son un - heard,
2. If in the dusk of the twi - light Dim be the re-gion a - far,

Hope, with a gen-tle per - sua - sion, Whis-pers her com-fort-ing word:
Will not the deep-en-ing dark - ness Bright-en the glim-mer-ing star?

Wait, till the dark-ness is o - ver, Wait till the tem-pest is done,
Then, when the night is up - on us, Why should the heart sink a - way?

Made in U.S.A.

Hope for the sun-shine to-mor - row, Af - ter the show-er is gone.___
When the dark mid-night is o - ver, Watch for the break-ing of day.___

REFRAIN

1-2. Whis - per-ing Hope,___ oh how wel - come thy voice,___

1-2. Whis-per-ing Hope, whis-per-ing Hope, wel-come thy voice, oh, how wel-come thy voice,

Mak - ing my heart___ in its sor - row re - joice.

Mak-ing my heart, mak-ing my heart in its sor - row re - joice.

Twinkle, Twinkle, Little Star

CHILDREN'S SONG

Arrgt. by Paul Hill

Twin-kle, twin-kle lit-tle star, How I won-der what you are
When the blaz-ing sun is gone, When he noth-ing shines up - on,

Up a - bove the world so high, Like a dia - mond in the sky
Then you show your lit - tle light, Twin-kle twin - kle all the night

Twin - kle, twin -kle, lit - tle star How I won - der what you are.

The Farmer In The Dell

CHILDREN'S SONG

Arrgt. by Paul Hill

Tune Uke
G C E A

1. The farm-er in the dell, the farm-er in the dell Heigh ho the der-ry oh, the farm-er in the dell.
2. The farm-er takes a wife, the farm-er takes a wife Heigh ho the der-ry oh, the farm-er takes a wife.
3. The wife takes a child, the wife takes a child Heigh ho the der-ry oh, the wife takes a child.

4. The child takes the nurse, etc.
5. The nurse takes the dog, etc.
6. The dog takes the cat, etc.

7. The cat takes the rat, etc.
8. The rat takes the cheese, etc.
9. The cheese stands alone, etc.

Lazy Mary, Will You Get Up

Arrgt. by Paul Hill

CHILDREN'S SONG

Tune Uke

G C E A

La - zy Mar - y will you get up, Will you get up, Will you get up.
No, no Moth-er, I won't get up, I won't get up, I won't get up

La - zy Mar - y will you get up, Will you get up to - day.
No no Moth - er, I - won't get up, I won't get up to - day.

Baa! Baa! Black Sheep

Arrgt. by Paul Hill

CHILDREN'S SONG

Tune Uke

G C E A

Baa! Baa! Black Sheep Have you an - y wool? Yes Sir, Yes Sir, Three bags full,

One for my mas - ter, And one for my dame, But none for the naugh-ty boy that cries in the lane.

Made in U.S.A.

'Round The Mulberry Bush

Simple Simon

3. This is the way we iron our clothes, etc.
So early Tuesday morning.

4. This is the way we scrub the floor, etc.
So early Wednesday morning.

5. This is the way we mend our clothes, etc.
So early Thursday morning.

6. This is the way we sweep the house, etc.
So early Friday morning.

7. This is the way we bake our bread, etc.
So early Saturday morning.

8. This is the way we go to church, etc.
So early Sunday morning.

Mary Had A Little Lamb

Arrgt. by Paul Hill

CHILDREN'S SONG

Little Bo Peep

Arrgt. by Paul Hill

CHILDREN'S SONG

Little Jack Horner

CHILDREN'S SONG

Arrgt. by Paul Hill

Little Boy Blue

CHILDREN'S SONG

Arrgt. by Paul Hill

Jack And Jill

Arrgt. by Paul Hill

CHILDREN'S SONG

Jack and Jill went up the hill, To fetch a pail of wa-ter;

Jack fell down and broke his crown and Jill came tum-b'ling af-ter.

Humpty Dumpty

Arrgt. by Paul Hill

CHILDREN'S SONG

Hum-pty Dum-pty sat on a wall, Hum-pty Dum-pty had a great fall,

All the kings hors-es and all the kings men Could-n't put Hum-pty to-geth-er a-gain.

America

SAMUEL F. SMITH

Arrgt. by Paul Hill

Star Spangled Banner

Arrgt. by Paul Hill

By FRANCIS SCOTT KEY

Oh say can you see By the dawn's ear-ly light, What so proud-ly we hailed at the twi-light's last
On the shore dim-ly seen, Thro' the mist of the deep, Where the foe's haughty host in dread si-lence re-

gleam-ing! Whose stripes and bright stars Thro' the per-il-ous fight, O'er the ram-parts we watched were so gal-lant-ly
pos-es What is that which the breeze, O'er the tow-er-ing steep As it fit-ful-ly blows, half conceals half dis-

stream-ing; And the rock-et's red glare, Bombs burst-ing in air, Gave proof thro' the night that our flag was still there. Oh!
clos-es? Now it catch-es the gleam of the morn-ings first beam, In full glo-ry re-flect-ed now shines in the stream. Oh!

say does that star span-gled ban-ner yet wave, O'er the land of the free, and the home of the brave.

Hail, Columbia

JOSEPH HOPKINSON

Arrgt. by Paul Hill

Yankee Doodle

Arrgt. by Paul Hill

La Marseillaise
National Anthem Of France

ROUGET DE LISLE

Arrgt. by Paul Hill

Tune Uke

A D F#B

Ye sons of free-dom, wake to glo - ry Hark! Hark! what my-riads bid you rise! Your chil-dren,

wives and grand-sires hoar - y, Be-hold their tears and hear their cries, Be-hold their tears and hear their

cries! Shall hate-ful ty - rants, mis-chief breed-ing, With hire-ling hosts a ruf-fian band, Af-fright and de-so-late the

land, When peace and lib-er-ty lie bleed-ing, To arms, to arms ye brave! Th'a veng - ing sword un-

sheath! March on, march on, All hearts_ re - solved_ on Lib - er-ty or death._

The Marseillaise
(French National Song)

French Verse

Allons enfants de la patrie,
Le jour de gloire est arrive!
Contre nous de la tyrannie
L'etendard sanglant est leve
L'etendard sanglant est leve
Entendez vous dans les campagnes
Mugir ces feroces soldats?
Ils viennent jusque dans nos bras
Egorger vos fils, vos compagnes:

Aux armes, citoyans! Formez vos bataillons!
Marchons, marchons, qu'un sang impur
A breuve nos sillons!

English Verse I

Now, now the dangerous storm is rolling
Which treach'rous Kings confed'rate, raise;
The dogs of war, let loose, are howling,
And lo! our fields and cities blaze;
And lo! our fields and cities blaze;
And shall we basely view the ruin,
While lawless force with guilty stride
Spreads desolation far and wide,
With crime and blood his hands embruing?

To arms! To arms! ye brave,
Th' avenging sword unsheathe;
March on! March on! All hearts resolved
On victory or death!

English Verse II

O liberty! can man resign thee,
Once having felt thy gen'rous flame?
Can dungeons, bolts or bars confine thee,
Or whips thy noble spirit tame?
Or whips thy noble spirit tame?
Too long the world has wept bewailing
That falsehood's dagger tyrants wield
But freedom is our sword and shield,
And all their arts are unavailing.

To arms! To arms! ye brave!
Th' avenging sword unsheathe;
March on! March on! All hearts resolved
On victory or death!

74

Dixie Land

Arrgt by Paul Hill

By DAN EMMET

Maryland, My Maryland

Arrgt. by Paul Hill

Andante

Thou wilt not cow - er in the dust, Mar - y-land, My Mar - y-land, Thy beam-ing sword shall
Thou wilt not yield the van-dal toll, Mar - y-land, My Mar - y-land, Thou wilt not crook to

nev - er rust Mar - y-land, My Mar - y-land Re mem-ber Car-roll's sa-cred trust; Re-
his con-trol, Mar - y-land, My Mar - y-land Bet - ter the fire up - on thee roll, Bet-

mem-ber How-ard's war-like thrust And all thy slumb'rers with the just Mar-y-land My Mar-y-land.
ter the shot the blade, the bowl, Than cru-ci-fix - ion of the soul Mar-y-land My Mar-y-land.

Tune Uke

A D F♯ B

Oh, My Darling Clementine

Arrgt. by Paul Hill

By P. MONTROSE

Made in U.S.A.

Polly Wolly Doodle

Arrgt. by Paul Hill

Marching Thru' Georgia

Arrgt. by Paul Hill

By HENRY C. WORK

Old Black Joe

Arrgt. by Paul Hill

STEPHEN C. FOSTER

Gone are the days   when my heart was young and gay   Gone are my friends, from the
Why do I weep,   when my heart should feel no pain   Why do I sigh   that my

cot - ton fields a - way;   Gone from the earth   to a   bet - ter land I know   I
friends come not a - gain.   Griev - ing for forms   now de - part - ed long a - go

hear their gen - tle voic - es call - ing "Old Black Joe."   I'm   com - ing, I'm com - ing, For my

head is bend - ing low,   I   hear those gen - tle voic - es call ing "Old Black Joe."

We're Tenting Tonight

WALTER KITTREDGE

Arrgt. by Paul Hill

Massa's In De Cold Ground

Arrgt. by Paul Hill

STEPHEN C. FOSTER

'Round de mead - ows a - ring - ing De dark - eys mourn - ful songs,
Where de i - vy am a - creep - ing O'er de gras - sy mound

While de mock-ing bird am sing - ing Hap-py as de day is long.
Dere old mas-sa am a - sleep - ing Sleep-ing in de cold cold ground.

Back in de corn - field Hear dat mourn - ful sound.

All de dark-ies am a - weep - ing Mas-sa's in de cold, cold ground.

Made in U.S.A.

My Old Kentucky Home

By STEPHEN FOSTER

Arrgt. by Paul Hill

Chorus

Weep no more, my la - dy Oh! weep no more, to - day! We will

sing one song, For my old Ken-tuck- y home, For my old Ken-tuck- y home, far a - way.

Arrgt. by Paul Hill

Tramp! Tramp! Tramp!

SOUTHERN PATRIOTIC SONG

GEO. F. ROOT

Tune Uke

F Bb D G

Tramp, tramp, tramp the boys are march -ing Cheer up, com-rades they will come And be-

neath the star- ry flag, We shall breathe the air a -gain, Of the free-land in our own be-lov-ed home.

A Home On The Range

Hallelujah - I'm A Bum

Arrgt. by Paul Hill

Oh, why don't you work like oth-er men do. How the
Oh, I love my boss and my boss loves me, And ___

hell can I work when there's no work to do.
that is I the rea-son ___ I'm so hun-gry.

Chorus

Hal-le-lu-jah I'm a bum, Hal-le-lu-jah, bum a-gain. Hal-le-

lu-jah give a hand out to re-vive us a-gain.

Made in U. S. A.

She'll Be Comin' 'Round The Mountain
(When She Comes)

Arrgt. by Paul Hill

HILL BILLY

Liebestraum
(Dream Of Love)

Music by
FRANZ LISZT

Made in U.S.A.

heart, To keep it shin - ing bright, _____ That

heart may an - swer heart in long em - brace. _____

loco

loco

Ah   Ah _ love! _____

That Big Rock Candy Mountain

Arrgt. by Paul Hill

On a sum-mer day in the month of May A bur-ly bum came hik-ing, Down a
On a run came a farm-er and his son to the hay fields they were bound-ing, Said the

shad-y lane thru the sug-ar cane He was look-ing for his lik-ing, As he roamed a-long he
bum to the son, "Why don't you come to that big rock can-dy moun-tain?" So the mail train stops and

sang a song of the land of milk and hon-ey— Where a bum can stay for man-y a day And he
there ain't no cops and the folks are ten-der count-ing— But they nev-er ar-rived at the lem-on-ade tide In that

Chorus

won't need an-y mon-ey— Oh, the buz-zin' of the bees in the cig-a-rette trees, Near the So-da wat-er
big rock can-dy moun-tain—

Made in U.S.A.

Hand Me Down My Walking Cane

The Letter Edged In Black

Tune Uke
F Bb D G

Arrgt. by Paul Hill

When The Work's All Done This Fall

Arrgt. by Paul Hill

HILL BILLY SONG

Lyric from a translation by
A. ASHLEY
Arrgt. by Paul Hill

Eli, Eli.

HEBREW SONG

E - li, E - li, _____ lo - ma, a sav - to - ni _____

E - li, E - li, _____ lo - ma, a sav - to - ni _____ In

fi - re and flame, we have been burned, — And per - se - cu - ted by all, and our head has been bow'd Our

God has been spurned And our ho - ly scroll dis - a - vowed Be - liefs have been mocked and our scroll de-

Kol Nidre
Prayer For The Day Of Atonement

Adaptation of Melody by
PAUL HILL

Arrgt. by Paul Hill

HEBREW CHANT

of none ef - fect. They shall not be bind - ing nor shall they have an - y pow - er. Our vows shall

not be vows Our bonds shall not be bonds And our oaths — shall not — be — oaths.

Solo

Hatikvoh
(The Hope)
Jewish Anthem

Arrgt. by PAUL HILL

Words & Music by L.N. IMBER

God Save The King

Arrgt. by Paul Hill

HENRY CAREY

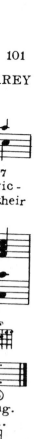

God save our gra-cious King Long live our no-ble King God save the King, Send him vic-
O, Lord our God a - rise, Scat-ter his en - e - mies And make them fall, Con-found their

to - ri - ous, Hap - py and glor - i - ous Long to reign o - ver us God save the King.
pol - i - tics, Frus-trate their knav-ish tricks On him our hopes we fix God save us all.

Bugle Calls

1. Assembly
2. Taps

Arrgt. by Paul Hill

1. Assembly

Tune Uke
G C E A

2. Taps

Tune Uke
G C E A

Comin' Thru The Rye

Arrgt. by Paul Hill

ROBERT BURNS

Blue Bells Of Scotland

Arrgt. by Paul Hill

SCOTCH SONG

Auld Lang Syne

Arrgt. by Paul Hill

ROBERT BURNS

My Bonnie

Arrgt. by Paul Hill

SCOTCH SONG

Tune Uke
G C E A

My Bon-nie lies o-ver the o-cean ___ My Bon-nie lies o-ver the sea; ___ My
Last night as I lay on my pil-low ___ Last night as I lay on my bed; ___ Last

Bon-nie lies o-ver the o-cean, ___ Oh, Bring back my Bon-nie to me. ___
night as I lay on my pil-low, ___ I dreamt that my Bon-nie was dead. ___

Bring back, Bring back, Bring back my Bon-nie to me to me.

Bring back, Bring back, Oh! Bring back my Bon-nie to me. ___

Annie Laurie

Arrgt. by Paul Hill

LADY SCOTT

Made in U. S. A.

Song Of The Volga Boatman

Tune Uke

F   Bb   D   G

Russian Folk Song
Arrgt. by Paul Hill

Two Guitars

Lyrics by
KERMIT LYONS
Arrgt: by Paul Hill

RUSSIAN FOLK SONG

Dark Eyes
(Otche Tchornia)

Lyrics by
KERMIT LYONS
Arrgt. by Paul Hill

RUSSIAN FOLK SONG

Tune Uke
A D F♯ B

Where the Vol - ga flows, A sweet Rus - sian rose
Rus - sian skies, We found Par - a - dise,

Set my soul a - flame, Son - ia was her name, Her dark
Then I sailed a - way, Leav - ing her to stay, Now a

flash - ing eyes, Seemed to hyp - no - tize, My heart missed a beat
vis - ion fair, Calls me to her there, And I re - a - lize

When we two would meet, Once heath the lure of her dark eyes.

Made in U.S.A.

La Paloma

Lyric by
KERMIT LYONS

Tune Uke
G C E A

Music by
SEBASTIAN YRADIER
Arrgt. by Paul Hill

Juanita

Words by
CAROLINE NORTON
Arrgt. by Paul Hill

SPANISH AIR

Tune Uke
F B♭ D G

Soft o'er the foun-tain, lin-g'ring falls the south-ern moon; Far o'er the
When in thy dream-ing, moons like those shall shine a - gain, And day-light

moun-tain, breaks the day too soon, In thy dark eyes splen-dor Where the warm light
beam-ing, prove thy dreams are vain; Wilt thou not, re - lent-ing For thine ab - sent

loves to dwell Wea-ry looks, yet ten-der speak their fond fare - well. Ni - ta Jua -
lov - er sigh! In thy heart con - sent-ing to a pray'r gone by. Ni - ta Jua -

ni-ta Ask thy soul if we should part Ni - ta Jua - ni-ta Lean thou on my heart.
ni-ta Let me lin-ger by thy side Ni - ta Jua - ni-ta Be my own fair bride.

Made in U.S.A.

La Golondrina
(The Swallow)

Arrgt. by Paul Hill

N. SARRADELL

Beautiful Heaven
Cielito Lindo

English Lyrics by
KERMIT LYONS
Arrgt. by Paul Hill

C. FERNANDEZ

Heav-ens a bove you all know that I love you, You
Bad times and fair, dear, I know you'll be there, dear, You'll

riv - al their beau - ty my darl -ing_____ I wait the
help me and guide me right_____ My heart is

day dear_____ When I can hear you say dear.
light _____ For I shall al - ways have you.

Chorus

I'll come to you_____ With loves own greet -ing_____ The
New days are nigh_____ Each one a glad day_____ We'll

Made in U.S.A.

Ay, Ay, Ay

Lyrics by
KERMIT LYONS
Arrgt by Paul Hill

CREOLE SONG

Tune Uke
A D F# B

stars a - bove will light up the way The heav-ens will bless our meet-ing.
both find joy and plea - sure un - told And nev - er know a sad day.

The love gleam-ing in your eyes Ay, Ay, Ay It's taunt-ing this poor heart of mine. Your eyes show me par-a -

dise, Ay. Ay, Ay, And fill me with pas-sion di - vine, I see you in all of my dreams, You're

taunt-ing me al-ways it seems, Oh tell me you love but me Ay, Ay, Ay Oh tell me you, love on-ly me.

El Choclo
Argentine Tango

Arrgt. by Paul Hill
Lyric by
KERMIT LYONS

A.G. VILLODO

I hold you close and gaze in-to your eyes so ten - der And look-ing there I find a mess-age of sur-

ren - der I see a prom-ise of a ma-gic night of ro - mance A per - fect

love dream seems to come to me as we dance If this___ tan-go and this night could last for-

ev - er With no to - mor-row we need fear our love to sev - er Then come what

may we'd know that love has come to stay _____ And you'll be mine my dar-ling for-e'er and a day.

Du, Du Liegst Mir Im Herzen

Arr. by PAUL HILL

GERMAN FOLK SONG

Lieber Augustin

Arr. by PAUL HILL

GERMAN FOLK SONG

Ich Liebe Dich
I Love Thee

Arrgt. by Paul Hill

EDVARD GRIEG

Thou art my thoughts, My pres-ent and my fu-ture, Thou art my
One thought of thee All oth-er thought drives from me, Pledged to thy

heart's su-preme, it's on-ly joy,_____ I love thee more than an-y earth-ly
good a-lone This heart shall be,_____ For to what-ev-er fate God's will may

crea-ture.⎱ I love thee dear, I love thee dear, I love thee now and for e-ter-ni-ty, I
doom me.⎰

love thee now and for e-ter-ni-ty.

Made in U.S.A.

Where Is My Little Dog Gone?
(Deutscher Dog)

Arrgt. by Paul Hill

GERMAN SONG

Oh where, oh where is my lit-tle dog gone, Oh where, oh where can he be?

With his ears cut short and his tail cut long, Oh where, oh where is he.

Today Is Monday

Arrgt. by Paul Hill

ARMY SONG

1. To-day is Mon - day   To-day is Mon - day   Mon-day bread and but-ter
2. To-day is Tues - day   To-day is Tues - day   Tues-day string beans
3. To-day is Wednes-day   To-day is Wednes-day   Wednesday soo - oo - p

All you hun - gry sol - diers   We wish the same to you.

4. Today is Thursday- Roast beef.
5. Today is Friday - Fish

6. Today is Saturday- Pay-day.
7. Today is Sunday - Church, ding dong.

Nelly Bly

Arr. by PAUL HILL

STEPHEN C. FOSTER

Nel-ly Bly, Nel-ly Bly bring de broom a-long, We'll sweep de kit-chen clean my dear, And hab a lit-tle song.
Poke de wood my lady lub, And make de fi - ah burn, And while I take de ban'-jo down, Just gib de musha turn.

Heigh, Nel-ly Ho! Nel-ly List-en, lub, to me, I'll sing for you, play for you A dul-cem mel-o-dy.

Old Dog Tray

Arr. by PAUL HILL

STEPHEN C. FOSTER

Old dog Tray's ev-er faith-ful Grief can-not drive him a - way He's

gen-tle, he is kind, I'll nev-er, nev-er find a bet-ter friend than old dog Tray.

The Wearing of the Green

Arr. by Paul Hill

Irish Song

ev - er you have seen They're hang-ing men and wom-en there for wear-ing of the green.

St. Patricks Day in the Morning

Lyric by
KERMIT LYONS
Arr. by Paul Hill

Irish Folk Song

Tune Uke

G C E A

Saint Pat-rick he chased all the snakes from the mire-land, chased all the snakes till there were
That's why we hon - or his name and we sing of him Sing of Saint Pat-rick with

1. none in Ire - land.

2. DANCE I - rish vim

Come Back To Erin

Arr. by Paul Hill

By CLARIBEL

Tune Uke

G C E A

1. Come back to Er-in, Ma-vour-neen, Ma-vour-neen, Come back a-roon to the land of thy birth,
2. O - ver the green sea, Ma-vour-neen, Ma-vour-neen, Long shone the white sail that bore thee a - way,

Come with the shamrocks and springtime, Ma-vour-neen, And it's Kil-lar-ney shall ring with our mirth. Sure when we sent thee to
Rid-ing the white waves that fair sum-mer morn-in' Just like a may flow'r a - float on the bay. O, but my heart sank, when

beau-ti - ful Eng-land, Lit-tle we thought of the lowe win-ter days, Lit-tle we thought of the hush of the star-ling,
clouds came be-tween us, Like a grey cur - tain the rain fall-ing down Hid from my sad eyes the path o'er the o -cean,

O-ver the moun-tain, the bluffs and the bays! Then come back to Er-in, Ma - vour-neen, Ma-vour-neen Come back a-gain to the
Far, far a - way where my Col- leen has flown

Copyright MCMXXXIII by Amsco Music Sales Co., N.Y. City
Made in U. S. A.

Rory O' More

Lyric by
KERMIT LYONS
Arr. by Paul Hill

Irish Song

Tune Uke

A D F# B

Dance

Copyright MCMXXXIII by Amsco Music Sales Co., N.Y. City
Made in U.S.A.

Killarney

Arrgt. by Paul Hill

M.W. BALFE

The Harp That Once Thro' Tara's Halls

THOMAS MOORE

Arrgt. by Paul Hill

1. The harp that once thro' Ta-ra's halls, The soul of mu-sic shed, Now hangs as mute on
2. No more to chiefs and la-dies bright, The harp of Ta-ra swells, The chord, a lone, that

Ta-ra's walls, As if that soul were fled, So sleeps the pride of for-mer days, So glo-ry's thrill is
breaks at night, It's tale of ruin tells. Thus free-dom now so sel-dom wakes, The on-ly throb she

o'er And hearts that once beat high for praise, Now feel that praise no more.
lives Is when some heart in-dig-nant breaks, To show that still she lives.

I'll Take You Home Again, Kathleen

Tune Uke
G C E A

THOMAS P. WESTENDORF
Arrgt. by Paul Hill

Would God I Were The Tender Apple Blossom

Arrgt. by Paul Hill

LONDONDERRY AIR

Would God I were the ten-der ap-ple blos-som That floats and falls from off the twist-ed bough,_ To lie and faint with-in your silk-en bos-om,With-in your silk-en bos-om at that does now! Or would I were a lit-tle bur-nish'd ap-ple, For you to pluck me glid-ing by so cold _ While sun and shade your robe of lawn will dap-ple, Your robe of lawn and your hair's spun gold._

Yea, would to God I were a-mong the ros-es That lean to kiss you as you flow be-tween,_While on the low-est branch a bud un-clo-ses, A bud un-clo-ses to touch you, Queen. **Nay** since you will not love, Would I were grow-ing A hap-py dai-sy in the gar-den path,_That so your sil-ver foot might press me go-ing, Might press me go-ing ev-en un-to death._

The Minstrel Boy

Arrgt. by Paul Hill

THOMAS MOORE

Highland Fling

Arrgt. by Paul Hill

Garry Owen

Arrgt. by Paul Hill

IRISH JIG

Made in U.S.A.

Fisher's Hornpipe

Arrgt. by Paul Hill

Tune Uke
G C E A

Emigrants Reel

Arrgt. by Paul Hill

REEL

Tune Uke
G C E A

Irish Washerwoman

Arrgt. by Paul Hill

JIG

Made in U.S.A.

Stack Of Barley

Sailor's Hornpipe

Arkansas Traveler

Arrgt. by Paul Hill

COUNTRY DANCE

Tune Uke
G C E A

Old Zip Coon
Turkey In The Straw

Arrgt. by Paul Hill

BUCK DANCE

Nelly Was A Lady

Arr. by PAUL HILL

STEPHEN FOSTER

The Spanish Cavalier

Arr. by PAUL HILL

MINSTREL SONG

The Campbells Are Coming

JIG

Arrgt. by Paul Hill

Pop Goes The Weasel

REEL

Arrgt. by Paul Hill

Paddy Whack

Arrgt. by Paul Hill

JIG

Where Did You Get That Hat?

Arrgt. by Paul Hill

Tune Uke
G C E A

Now, how I came to get this hat, 'Tis very strange and funny; My grand father died and left to me his property and money; And

when the will it was read out, they told me straight and flat; If I would have his mon-ey I must al-ways wear this hat

Chorus

Where did you get that hat? Where did you get that tile? Is-n't it a nob-by one, And just the pro-per style;

I should like to have one just the same as that! Where e'er I go they shout "Hel-lo, where did you get that hat?"

Madamoiselle From Armentiers
(Hinky Dinky Parlee Voo)

Arrgt. by Paul Hill

Down Went McGinty

Arrgt. by Paul Hill

Frankie And Johnny

Arrgt. by Paul Hill

Tune Uke
G C E A

1. Frank-ie and John-ny were lov-ers, Oh, Lord-y how they could love. They swore to be true to each
2. Frank-ie and John-ny went walk-ing, John-ny in his brand new suit. Oh good Lord says

oth-er, True as the stars a-bove, He was her man, _____ But he done her wrong. So wrong.
Frank-ie, Don't my John-ny look cute, He was her man, _____ But he done her wrong. So wrong.

3. Johnny said I've got to leave you,
But I won't be very long
Don't you wait up for me honey,
Nor worry while I'm gone
He was her man, but he done her wrong.

4. Frankie went down to the corner,
Stopped in to buy her some beer
Says to the fat bar-tender
Has my Johnny man been here
He was her man, but he done her wrong.

5. "Well I ain't going to tell you no story,
Ain't going to tell you no lie.
Johnny went by, 'bout an hour ago,
With a girl named Nellie Blye,
He was your man, but he's doin' you wrong.

6. Frankie went home in a hurry,
She didn't go there for fun,
She hurried home to get a hold,
Of Johnny's shootin' gun
He was her man, but he's doin' her wrong.

7. Frankie took a cab at the corner,
Says "Driver, step on this can."
She was just a desperate woman,
Gettin' two-timed by her man.
He was her man, but he's doin' her wrong.

8. Frankie got out at South Clark Street,
Looked in a window so high
Saw her Johnny man a lovin' up,
That high brown Nellie Blye
He was her man, but he's doin' her wrong.

9. Johnny saw Frankie a comin',
Out the back door he did scoot,
But Frankie took aim with her pistol,
And the gun went root a toot-toot
He was her man, but he done her wrong.

10. Oh roll me over so easy,
Roll me over so slow,
Roll me over easy boys,
'Cause my wounds they hurt me so
I was her man, but I done her wrong.

11. Bring out your long black coffin,
Bring out your funeral clo'es,
Johnny's gone and cashed his checks,
To the grave-yard Johnny goes.
He was her man, but he done her wrong.

12. Drive out your rubber tired carriage,
Drive out your rubber tired hack
There's twelve men going to the grave-yard,
And eleven coming back
He was her man, but he done her wrong.

13. The sheriff arrested poor Frankie,
Took her to jail that same day
He locked her up in a dungeon cell,
And threw the key away,
She shot her man, though he done her wrong

Made in U.S.A.

What The **** Do We Care

Arrgt. by Paul Hill

ARTHUR SULLIVAN

The Old Gray Mare

Arrgt. by Paul Hill

The Man Who Broke The Bank At Monte Carlo

Arrgt. by Paul Hill

As I walk a-long the Bois Boo-long, With an in-de-pen-dent air — You can hear the girls de-clare —"He must be a mil-lion-aire"— You can hear them sigh and wish to die, You can see them wink the oth-er eye, At the man that broke the bank at Mon-te Car - lo.

Tune Uke
A D F#B

Git Along Little Doggies

COWBOY SONG

Arrgt. by Paul Hill

Whop-pee Ti Yi Yo— Git a-long lit-tle dog-gies, It's your mis-for-tune And none of my own, Whoo-pee

Tune Uke
A D F#B

Ti Yi Yo Git a-long lit-tle dog-gies You know that Wy-om-ing will be your new home.

Abdul, The Bulbul Ameer

Arrgt. by Paul Hill

Tune Uke

G C E A

1 The sons of the pro-phet are har-dy and bold And quite un-ac-cus-tomed to
2 There are he-roes in plen-ty and well known to fame, In the ranks that are led by the
want-ed a man to en-cour-age the van Or to shout hulla-loo in the
Ti-mi-thie Irv-ing, play euc-her or pool, And per-form on the Span-ish Gui-

fear,___ But of all the most reck-less of life or or limb was Ab-dul the Bul-bul A-
rear,___ Or to storm a re-doubt They straight way sent out for Ab-dul the Bul-bul A-
Czar,___ But a-mong the most reck-less of name or of fame was I-van Pet-ru-ski Ski-
tar,___ In fact quite the cream of the Mos-co-vite team was I-van Pet-ru-ski Ski-

1. meer___ When they meer.___ For Ab-dul the Bul-bul A... meer.
2. vah___ He could vah.___ Was I-van Pet-ru-ski Ski-vah.

Fair Harvard

COLLEGE SONG

Arrgt. by Paul Hill

John Brown's Body

Arrgt. by Paul Hill

W. STEFFE

Solomon Levi

Arrgt. by Paul Hill

O Sol-o-mon Le-vi! Le-vi tra la la la _____ Poor Sol-lie Le-vi! tra la la la la la la la la la la My name is Sol-o-mon Le-vi, At my store on Sa-lem Street, _____ That's where you'll buy your coats and vests and ev-'ry-thing else that's neat _____ I've sec-ond hand-ed Ul-ster's and ev-'ry-thing else that's

fine. — For all the boys they trade with me At a hun-dred and for-ty nine. —

Upidee

Arrgt. by Paul Hill

COLLEGE SONG

Tune Uke

A D F#B

The shades of night were fall-ing fast, Tra la la tra, la la As through a moun-tain vil-lage passed
His brow was sad, his eye be-neath, Tra la la tra, la la Flashed like a fal-chion from it's sheath

Tra la la la la A youth who bore 'mid snow and ice, A ban-ner with a strange de-vice.
Tra la la la la And like a sil-ver clar-ion rung, The ac-cents of that un-known tongue.

U-pi-dee I dee I da U-pi-dee u-pi-da U-pi-dee I dee I da U-pi-dee i da.

Made in U.S.A.

Ah! So Pure
From "Martha"

Arrgt. by Paul Hill

F. Von FLOTOW

Moderato

Ah! so pure Ah! so bright, burst her beau - ty on my

bright. Oh! so mild so di - vine_____ She be-guiled this heart of mine.

Mar - tha, Mar - tha, thou hast tak - en, ev - 'ry bliss a - way with thee.

Cans't thou leave me, thus for sak - en Come and share thy boon with me.

Ah! I Have Sighed To Rest Me

From 'Il Travatore"

Arrgt. by Paul Hill

Andante sostenuto

G. VERDI

Belle Nuit, O Nuit D'Amour

Barcarolle
From "Tales of Hoffmann"

English Lyrics by
KERMIT LYONS

Arr. by Paul Hill

JACQUES OFFENBACH

Then You'll Remember Me

From "The Bohemian Girl"

Arrgt. by Paul Hill

M. W. BALFE

Andante cantabile

Wher oth - er lips and oth - er___ hearts, their tales of love shall
When cold - ness or de - ceit shall___ slight, the beau - ty now they

tell In lan-guage whose ex - cess im - parts, the pow'r they feel so well; There
prize, And deem it but a fa - ded light, which beams with-in your eyes; When

may per -haps in such___ a ___ scene, Some rec - o - lec - tion be, _____ Of days that have as
hol - low hearts shall wear___ a ___ mask,'Twill break your own to see _____ In such a mo-ment

hap - py___ been, And you'll re - mem - ber me_____ And you'll re - mem-ber,You'll re -mem ber me.
I but___ ask, That you'll re - mem - ber me_____ That you'll re - mem-ber,You'll re -mem ber me.

Made in U.S.A.

Lullaby
From "Jocelyn"

Lyrics by
KERMIT LYONS
Arrgt. by Paul Hill

BENJAMIN GODARI

That song it's tone so clear. Just seem to bring my loved one near.

The Last Rose Of Summer

Words by
THOMAS MOORE
Arrgt. by Paul Hill

From "Martha"

VON FLOTOW

'Tis the last rose of sum-mer, Left bloom-ing a - lone; All her love-ly com-
I'll not leave thee, thou lone one, To pine on the stem, Since the love-ly are

pan - ions, Are fad - ed and gone; No flow - er of her kin-dred, No
sleep-ing, Go sleep thou with them, Thus kind - ly I scat-ter thy

rose bud is nigh ___ To re - flect back her blush-es, or give sigh for sigh
leaves o'er the bed; ___ Where thy mates of the gar-den, lie scent - less and dead

Made in U. S. A.

Bridal Chorus
(From the opera "Lohengrin")

Lyric by
KERMIT LYONS
Arrgt. by Paul Hill

Music by
RICHARD WAGNER

Faith-ful and true, we lead you forth Where love tri-
Star of re-nown, flow'r of the earth May your young

umph - ant, shall crown you with joy! Star of re-nown, flow'r of the
love know but glad-ness and mirth Here comes the bride, heart filled with

earth May your young love know but glad-ness and mirth.
pride Here comes the groom, may love with them a - bide

Fine

Cham-pion vic-tor-ious go thou be-fore! Maid, bright and glo-rious, go thou be-fore!

D.S.

Woman Is Fickle
(Rigoletto)

Arrgt. by Paul Hill

G. VERDI

Tune Uke
A D F#B

Wom-an is fick-le False al-to-geth-er Moves like a feath-er,
Wretch-ed the day is When she looks kind-ly Trusts to her blind-ly,

Borne on the breez-es Wom-an with witch-ing smile will e'er de-ceive you, Oft-en will
Her life thus wast-ing Yet she must sure-ly be dull be-yond meas-ure, Who of love's

grieve you, Yet as she pleas-es Her heart's un-feel-ing False al-to-geth-er
hap-pi-ness: Ne'er has been tast-ing, Wom-an's un-feel-ing False al-to-geth-er

poco

Moves like a feath-er Borne on the breeze.   Borne on the breeze.
Moves like a feath-er Borne on the breeze.   Borne on the breeze.

Sextette
From the opera "Lucia Di Lammermoor"

GAETANO DONIZETTI

Arrgt. by Paul Hill

Copyright MCMXXXIII by Amsco Music Sales Co., N.Y. City
Made in U.S.A.

Habanera
from the Opera "Carmen"

Arrgt. by Paul Hill

GEORGES BIZET

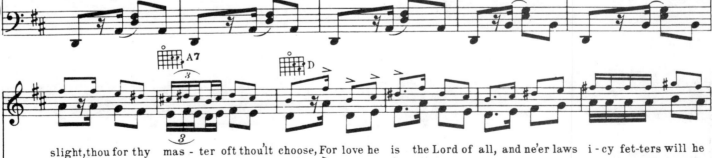

Ah! love, thou art a wil-ful wild bird, and none may hope thy wings to tame, If it
pray'rs a-like un-heed-ing, oft ar-dent hom-age thou'lt re-fuse, Whilst

please thee to be a reb-el, say who can try and thee re - claim? Threats and
he who doth cold-ly slight, thou for thy mas-ter oft thou'lt   choose, Threats and

pray'rs a-like un-heed-ing oft ar-dent hom - age thou'lt re - fuse,   Whilst   he who doth cold-ly

slight, thou for thy mas - ter oft thou'lt choose, For love he is the Lord of all, and ne'er laws i - cy fet-ters will he

wear, It thou me lov-est not, I love thee, And if I love thee, now be-ware! Love thou not me, Then I love

thee and if I love thee now be ware! Love thou not me, Then I love thee and if I love thee, now be - ware!__

Lullaby
from the Opera "Ermine"

Arrgt. by Paul Hill

ED. JAKOBOWSKI

Dear Moth-er in dreams I see her, With loved face sweet and calm,— And hear her voice with

love re-joice, When nest-ling on her arm.__ I think how she soft-ly pressed me, Of the

tears in each glis-t'ning eye,___ As her watch she'd keep when she rocked to sleep, This

ten-der sweet lul-la-by:___ "Bye, bye, bye, bye, bye, bye, bye, bye, Bye, bye, bye, bye, bye, bye;"___

L'istesso tempo

"Bye, bye, drow-si-ness o'er-tak-ing, Pret-ty lit-tle eye-lids sleep,___

Bye, bye,___ watch-ing till thou'rt wak-ing, Dar-ling, be thy slum-ber deep!"___

Heavenly Aïda

From the Opera "Aïda"

Arr'gt by Paul Hill

GIUSEPPE VERDI

Andante espressivo

Heav'n - ly_ A - ï - da beau - ty_ re - splen - dent Ra - di - ant flow - er,

bloom ing_ and bright Queen - ly_ thou reign - est o'er me tran-

scend-ent, Bathing my spirit in beau-ty's light. Would that thy

bright_ skies once more be hold - ing, Breath ing the soft airs of thy na - tive land Round thy fair

Copyright MCMXXXIII by Amsco Sales Co., N.Y. City
Made in U.S.A.

Toreador Song
From the Opera "Carmen"

Arr'gt by Paul Hill

G. BIZET

Marziale

Tune Uke
G C E A

brow a di-a-dem fold-ing, Thine were a throne ___ next the sun to stand!

Tor - e - a-dor, e'er watch-ful be   Tor - e - a-dor   Tor - e - a-dor

Don't ___ for-get the bright-est of eyes, Fond-ly thee a - wait ___

And ___ love's the prize for thee, Tor - e - a-dor And love's the prize for thee!

Evening Star
From the opera "Tannhäuser"

Arrgt. by Paul Hill

RICHARD WAGNER

Roll Jordan Roll

NEGRO SPIRITUAL

Arrgt. by Paul Hill

Red River Valley

Arrgt. by Paul Hill

Slowly

From this val - ley they say you are go - ing — We will
Won't you think of the val - ley you're leav - ing — Oh, how

Somebody's Knocking At Your Door

Arrgt. by Paul Hill

SPIRITUAL

Tune Uke

F Bb D G

Go Down Moses

Arrgt. by Paul Hill

SPIRITUAL

Tune Uke
G C E A

an-swer, Some-bod-y's knock-ing at your door.

Go down Mos-es 'Way down in E-gypt land Tell ole Pha-roah

Let my peo-ple go. When go. Is-real was in E-gypt land Let my peo-ple

to next strain Fine

go Op-pressed so hard they could not stand Let my peo-ple go.

D.S. al Fine

Heav'n, Heav'n

Arrgt. by Paul Hill

NEGRO SPIRITUAL

Nobody Knows The Trouble I've Seen

Arrgt. by Paul Hill

NEGRO SPIRITUAL

Made in U.S.A.

Deep River

Arrgt. by Paul Hill

NEGRO SPIRITUAL

Swing Low, Sweet Chariot

Arrgt. by Paul Hill

NEGRO SPIRITUAL

Tune Uke

A D F♯ B

Climbing Up The Golden Stairs

Arr. by Paul Hill

Jesus, Lover Of My Soul

Arrgt. by Paul Hill

S. B. MARSH

SACRED HYMN

Jes - us lov - er of my soul Let me to Thy bos - om fly
Oth - er re - fuge have I none Hangs my help - less soul on Thee.

While the wear - er wat - ers roll, While the temp - est still is high.
Leave, Ah! leave me not a - lone, Still sup - port and com - fort me!

Hide me, O my Sav - ior hide. 'Till the storm of life be past.
All my trust on Thee is stayed.- All my help from Thee I bring,-

Safe in - to the hav - en guide Oh re - ceive my soul at last.
Cov - er my de - fense - less head With the shad - ows of Thy wing.

Made in U. S. A.

It Came Upon The Midnight Clear
Sacred Song

EDMUND H. SEARS
Arrgt. by Paul Hill

RICHARD S. WILLIS

XMAS SONG

It came up-on the mid-night clear, That glor-ious song of old From an-gels bend-ing near the earth, To touch their harps of gold. ___ "Peace on the earth, Good will to men, From Heav'ns all grac-ious King." The world in sol-emn still-ness lay to hear the an-gels sing.

Still through the clo-ven skies they come, With peace-ful wings un-furl'd; And still their Heav'n-ly mu-sic floats O'er all the wear-y world. ___ A-bove it's sad and low-ly plains, They bend on hov-'ring wing. And ev-er o'er it's ba-bel sounds the bless-ed an-gels sing.

Copyright MCMXXXIII by Amsco Music Sales Co., N.Y.C.

Made in U.S.A.

Rocked In The Cradle Of The Deep

J. P. KNIGHT

Arrgt. by Paul Hill

Copyright MCMXXXIII by Amsco Music Sales Co., N.Y.C.

Lead Kindly Light

Arrgt. by Paul Hill

By J.B. DYKES

SACRED
SONG

calm and peace-ful is my sleep, — Rock'd in the crad-le of the deep.

Lead kind-ly light, A-mid th'en-cir-cling gloom.— Lead Thou me on; The night is
I was not ev-er thus, Nor pray'd that Thou— Shouldst lead me on; I loved to

dark and I am far from home, Lead Thou me on — Keep Thou my feet; I
choose and see my path, But now— Lead Thou me on — I loved the gar-ish

do not ask— to— see The dis-tant scene; One step e-nough for me,
day and spite— of— fears Pride ruled my will! Re-mem-ber not— past years.—

Cantique De Noel
(O Holy Night)

Arrgt. by Paul Hill

A. ADAM

Oh ho - ly night the stars are bright-ly shin - ing, It is the night of the dear Sav-iours
Led by the light of faith se-rene-ly beam - ing, With glow-ing hearts by His cra-dle we

birth Long lay the world in sin and er - ror pin - ing Till He ap-pear'd and the soul felt His
stand; So led by light of star so sweet-ly gleam - ing Here came the wise men from the O'- rient

worth A thrill of hope The wear-y world re-joi - ces For yon-der breaks a
land. The King of Kings Thus lay in low-ly man-ger In all our tri - als

new and glo-rious morn Fall on your knees! Oh hear _____ the an - gel
born to be our friend He knows our needs, To our _____ weak-ness no

Made in U.S.A.

voi - ces Oh, night ____ di - vine Oh, night ____ when Christ was born Oh
stran - ger Be - hold ____ your King Be - fore ____ Him low - ly bend Be -

night ____ di - vine oh night, oh night di - vine.
hold ____ your King, your King Be - fore Him bend.

The Lord's Prayer

Arrgt. by Paul Hill

SACRED CHANT

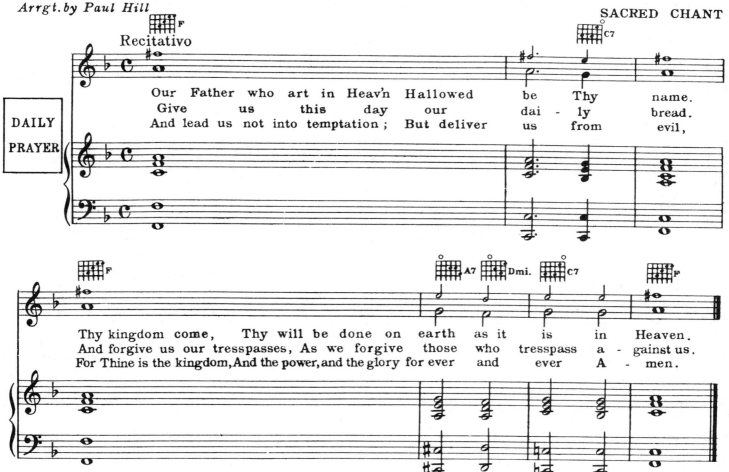

Recitativo

DAILY PRAYER

Our Father who art in Heav'n Hallowed be Thy name.
Give us this day our dai - ly bread.
And lead us not into temptation; But deliver us from evil,

Thy kingdom come, Thy will be done on earth as it is in Heaven.
And forgive us our tresspasses, As we forgive those who tresspass a - gainst us.
For Thine is the kingdom, And the power, and the glory for ever and ever A - men.

Onward, Christian Soldiers

Arrgt. by Paul Hill

SIR ARTHUR SULLIVAN

SACRED MARCH

On ward, chris-tian sol - diers, March - ing as to war; With the cross of
Like a might - y ar - my, Moves the church of God; Broth-ers, we are

Je - sus, Go - ing on be - fore; Christ the roy - al mas - ter, Leads a -gainst the
tread - ing, Where the saints have trod. We are not di - vid - ed All one bod - y

foe; For - ward in - to bat - tle See His ban - ners go,
we, One in hope and doc - trine, One in char - i - ty.

On-ward, chris-tian sol - diers March-ing as to war. With the cross of Je-sus Go-ing on be-fore.

Made in U. S. A.

O, Come, All Ye Faithful
Adeste Fidelis

REV. F. OAKELEY
Arrgt. by Paul Hill

J, READING

The Lost Chord

Arrgt. by Paul Hill

By SIR ARTHUR SULLIVAN
and ADELAIDE A. PROCTOR

Copyright MCMXXXIII by Amsco Music Sales Co., N.Y. City Made in U.S.A. *All Rights Reserved*

Calvary

Arrgt. by Paul Hill

PAUL RODNEY

Copyright MCMXXXIII by Amsco Music Sales Co., N.Y. City

Ave Maria

Words Revised by
KERMIT LYONS
Simplified
Arrgt. by Paul Hill

BACH-GOUNOD

SACRED
SONG

Ave Maria

FRANZ SCHUBERT

Arrgt. by Paul Hill

SACRED SONG

Tres lento

A - ve Ma-ri - a maid - en mild Oh list - en to a maid - en's pray - er! For thou canst hear tho' from the wild And thou canst save a-mid de-spair A - mid de-spair Safe may we sleep be - neath thy care tho'

Made in U.S.A.

ban - ish'd out-cast and re-viled   O maid - en! hear a maid-en's pray - er

moth - er___ hear a sup-pli-ant child.

Solo

Battle Hymn Of The Republic

Arrgt.by Paul Hill

W. STEFFE &
JULIA WARD HOWE

Silent Night! Holy Night!
(Stille Nacht! Heilige Nacht!)

Lyrics by
KERMIT LYONS
Arr. by Paul Hill

FRANZ GRUBER

The Lord Is My Shepherd

Arr. by Paul Hill

Sacred Chant

Rock Of Ages
Sacred Song

Arr. by Paul Hill

THOMAS HASTINGS

Nearer, My God, To Thee

Arr. by Paul Hill

LOWELL MASON